Travelling

Gill Tanner and Tim Wood

Photographs by Maggie Murray

Illustrations by Mark Peppé

A & C Black · London

Here are some of the people you will meet in this book.

The Miller Family in 1990

The Grant Family in 1960

Alan Miller

Helen Miller

Jane

Tony

Peter Grant

Rose Grant

Terry

Debbie

Helen

Tony Miller is the same age as you.
His sister, Jane, is eight years old.
What is Tony's mum called?

This is Tony's mum, Helen,
when she was nine years old, in 1960.
She is with her mum and dad,
her brother and her baby sister.

The Brown Family in 1930

The Jennings Family in 1900

Victoria Brown
Robert Brown
Emma
Rose and John

Anna Jennings
Thomas Jennings
Joe
Sam
Mary
Victoria
Edward

This is Tony's granny, Rose, when she was just a baby, in 1930. Her brother, John, is looking after her.

This is Tony's great grandma, Victoria, when she was six years old, in 1900. Can you see what her brothers and her sister are called?

Can you spot the differences
between these two pictures?

One shows a modern city street
and one shows a city street
one hundred years ago.

This book is about travelling.

It will help you find out how
travel has changed
in the last hundred years.

There are twelve mystery objects
in this book and you can find out
what they are.
They will tell you a lot
about people in the past.

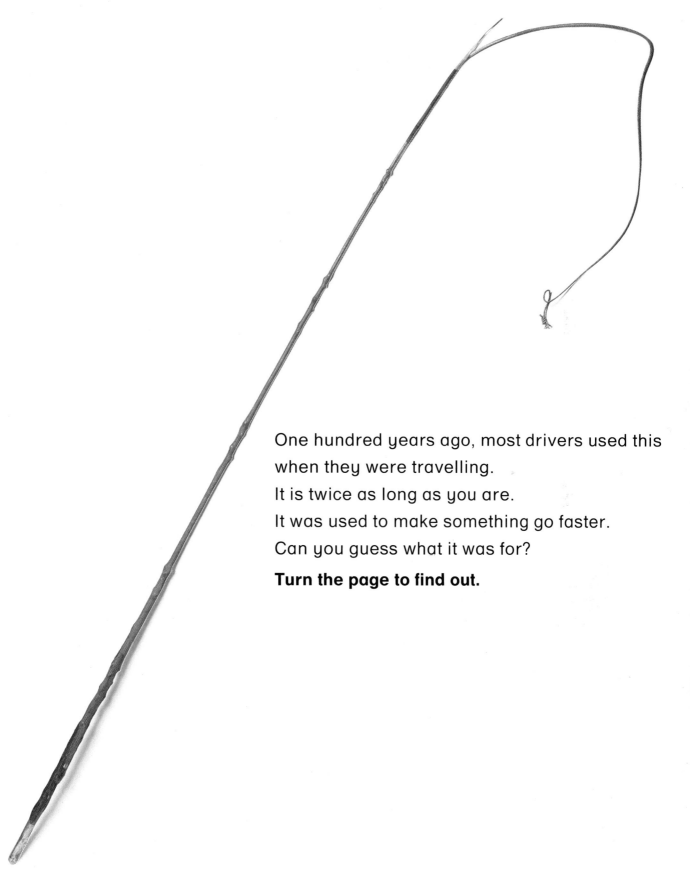

One hundred years ago, most drivers used this
when they were travelling.

It is twice as long as you are.

It was used to make something go faster.

Can you guess what it was for?

Turn the page to find out.

Can you find the mystery object in this picture?
It's a **driving whip**.
In those days most buses, trams, cabs and carts
were pulled by horses.
The drivers used whips to make the horses
go faster and to show other drivers
which way they were going to turn.

When Mr Jennings returned from a long train journey
he took a hansom cab home from the railway station.
He told the driver where to go
by speaking through a little trapdoor in the roof.
When the cab arrived at his house, he paid the driver.

This mystery object is nearly as tall as a page of this book.

Mr and Mrs Jennings both had one.

It was very useful when they wanted to travel about at night.

What do you think it is made of?

Turn the page to find out what it is.

Mr and Mrs Jennings are returning
from a day out with their cycling club.

Can you spot the mystery object?
It's a **bicycle lamp**.

The light was made by gas inside the lamp.
The gas was quite dangerous,
but in those days people couldn't buy lamps which worked by batteries.

Cycling clubs were very popular in 1900.
The club members went on long rides into the countryside
for sight-seeing and picnics.

8

This mystery object is as long as one of your arms.
Does it remind you of a musical instrument?
Look very closely.
See if you can guess how it worked.
Turn the page to find out what it is.

Mary and Sam were excited to see a motor car in their street.
Can you spot the mystery object?
It's a **motor car horn**.
The driver squeezed the round, rubber bulb
and the horn made a noise something like a trumpet.

Motor cars had only just been invented in 1900.
They were very expensive and only rich people could afford them.
Servants, called chauffeurs, drove the cars and kept them clean.
In those days, motor cars often broke down,
so chauffeurs had to know how to repair the cars.

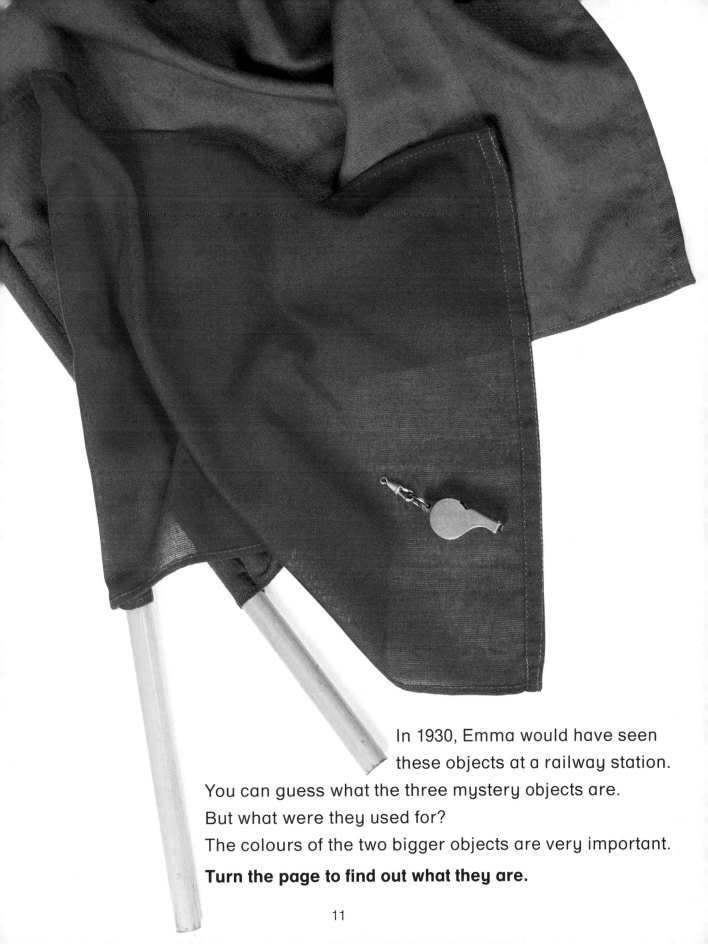

In 1930, Emma would have seen these objects at a railway station.
You can guess what the three mystery objects are.
But what were they used for?
The colours of the two bigger objects are very important.

Turn the page to find out what they are.

This is Emma Brown and her parents at a railway station in 1930.
Emma Brown is going to visit her auntie.
Can you spot the mystery objects?
They are the **guard's flags** and **whistle**.

The guard waved the green flag and blew his whistle
when it was time for the train to leave the station.
He waved the red flag to tell the driver to stop the train.

TRAIN DEPAR

10:00

What do you think these mystery objects are?

The larger one is made of wood.

It is about as long as a page of this book.

The smaller one is made of metal.

It is about the same size as a pair of scissors.

Can you guess what they were used for?

Turn the page to find out.

The mystery objects are a **ticket clip** and a **pair of clippers**.
When Victoria Brown took her children on a bus,
she paid the fares to a conductor.

The conductor gave her tickets from the ticket clip.
John and Emma travelled half-price, so their tickets
were a different colour from their mother's.
The inspector used the clippers to punch a hole
in each ticket.

This mystery object is made of metal.

It is about as long as your arm.

In the 1930s all cars had one of these.

What do you think it was used for?

Turn the page to find out.

In 1930, cars were much cheaper than they had been
when Victoria Brown was a child.
More people could afford to buy them.
Mr Brown was taking his family on holiday
in their little car.
Can you spot the mystery object?
It's a **starting handle**.

The electric starter did not always work.
Mr Brown pushed the starting handle into the engine
through a hole in the front of the car.
He turned the handle round and round to start the engine.

16

In 1960, Peter Grant travelled to work on a motorbike.
It was quicker than going by car or bus.
He was not held up in traffic jams
and he could park his bike easily in town.

While he rode he wore this mystery object.
Can you guess what it is? **Turn the page to find out.**

This is the street where the Grants lived in 1960.
How is it different from your street?
Can you spot the mystery object?
It's a **pair of goggles**.

When Peter Grant rode his motorbike
the goggles kept the wind and dust out of his eyes.
He wore a crash helmet to protect his head.
Not long after this, a law was passed
to make all motorcyclists wear crash helmets.

This mystery object is about as big as your head.

It is made of plastic and lit up at night.

It is part of something much bigger.

What do you think it is?

Turn the page to find out.

Can you spot the mystery object?
It's the top of a **petrol pump**.

WEST END SERV

ESSO POPULAR

ESSO POPULAR

AJK 403

WAS
Whi
w

Rose Grant owned a Mini car.
When she needed petrol, she went to a garage.
In those days, most garages were quite small.
There weren't many self-service garages,
the petrol pumps were worked by one of the garage staff.

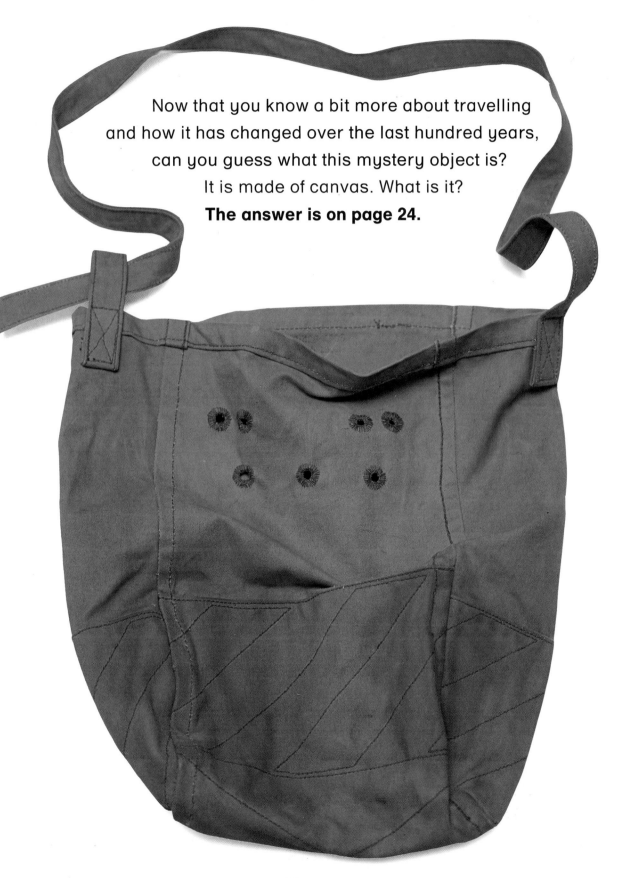

Now that you know a bit more about travelling
and how it has changed over the last hundred years,
can you guess what this mystery object is?
It is made of canvas. What is it?

The answer is on page 24.

Time-line

These pages show you the kinds of transport in this book and the transport we use nowadays.

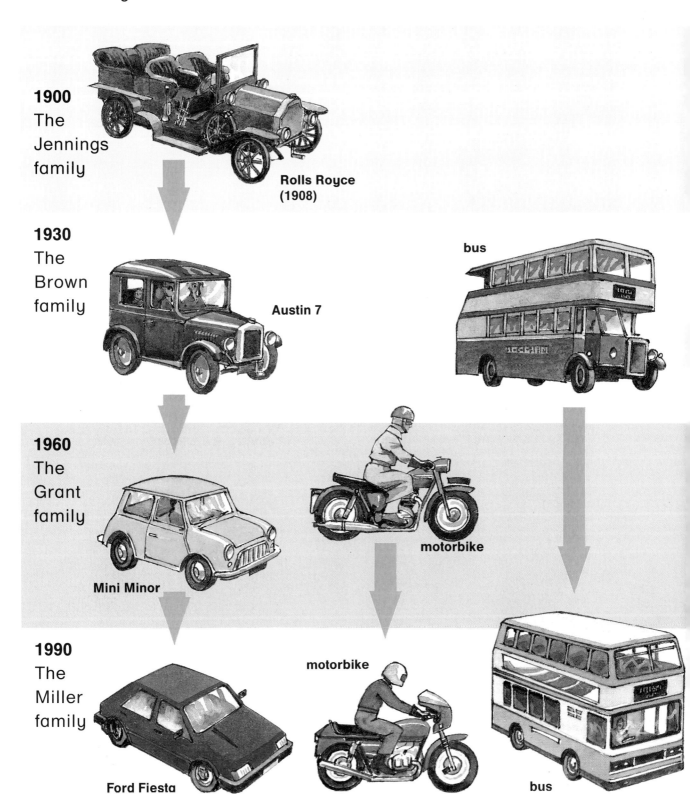

1900
The Jennings family

Rolls Royce (1908)

1930
The Brown family

Austin 7

bus

1960
The Grant family

Mini Minor

motorbike

1990
The Miller family

Ford Fiesta

motorbike

bus

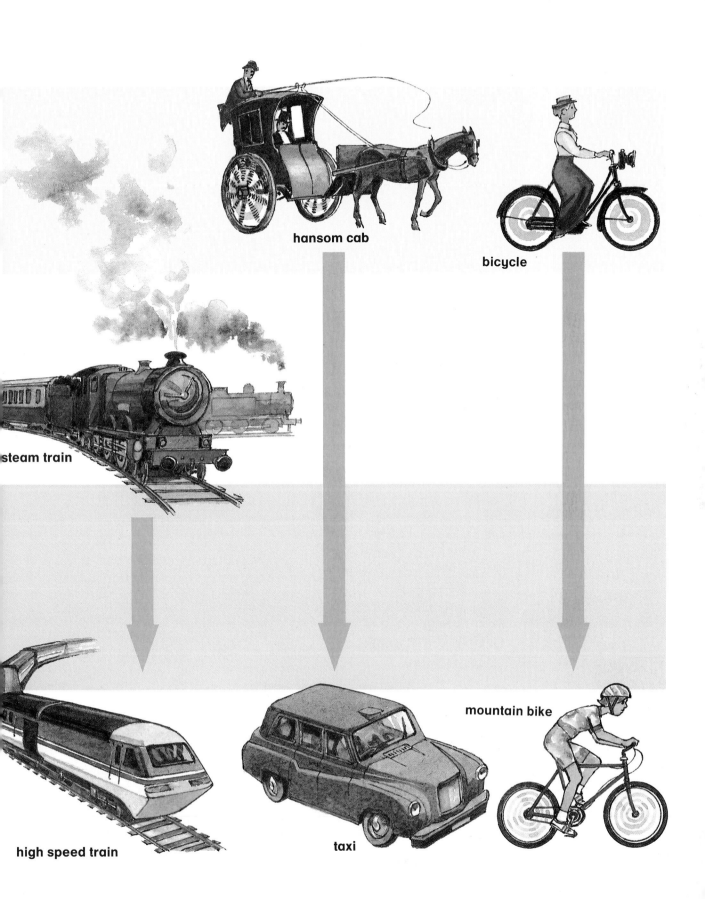

hansom cab

bicycle

steam train

mountain bike

high speed train

taxi

Index

The **mystery object** on page 21 was a **nosebag** used when Victoria Jennings was a child. The bag pulled over a horse's nose so the horse could eat while still harnessed.

For parents and teachers

More about the objects and pictures in this book

Pages 5/6 The Jennings family lived in a large industrial town. Hansom cabs were used like modern taxis and could be caught at a cab rank or hailed in the street.

Pages 7/8 Bikes in 1900 were quite similar to modern versions. Cycling became a craze after 1890, with the invention of the pneumatic tyre which made bikes more comfortable.

Pages 9/10 In 1930, petrol had to be bought at a chemist's shop. The speed limit (1903–31) on all roads was 20 mph. If the horn was sounded before an accident, a magistrate was unlikely to convict the driver!

Pages 11/12 The Browns lived in a semi-detached house in a small town. In 1930, all locomotives (except on the London underground which was electrified in 1890) were driven by steam. The first diesel trains were introduced in 1931 and the first electric line (London–Brighton) opened in 1933.

Pages 13/14 In 1930, each bus had a driver and a conductor. The last horse-drawn bus stopped running in 1916.

Pages 15/16 Electric starters were unreliable in 1930 because batteries went flat easily. The handle was often used on cold mornings.

Pages 17/18 The Grants lived in one of the new towns built in the 1960s. There were about a million motorbikes in Britain in 1960, mostly British. Crash helmets became compulsory in 1972.

Pages 19/20 The first automatic petrol pump was introduced in Britain in 1921 in Manchester. Self-service stations were almost unknown until the opening of the M1 in 1960.

Things to do

History Mysteries will provide an excellent starting point for all kinds of history work. There are a lot of general ideas which can be drawn out of the pictures, particularly in relation to the way houses, clothes, family size and lifestyles have changed in the last 100 years. Below are some starting points and ideas for follow up activities:

1 Work on families and family trees can be developed from the family on pages 2/3, bearing in mind that many children do not come from two-parent, nuclear families. Why do the families in the books have different surnames even though they are related? How have their clothes and hair styles changed over time?

2 Find out more about travel in the past from a variety of sources, including interviews with older people in the community, magazines, books, museums and manufacturers' information. Travel wasn't the same for everyone. Why not?

3 There is one object which is in one picture of the 1900s, one picture of the 1930s, and one picture of the 1960s. Can you find it?

4 Make a local study about transport near your school and/or a field trip to a railway preservation society.

5 Look at the difference between the photographs and the illustrations in this book. What different kinds of things can they tell you?

6 Make your own collection of travel objects or pictures. You can build up an archive or school museum over several years by encouraging children to bring in old objects, collecting unwanted items from parents, collecting from junk shops and jumble sales. You may also be able to borrow handling collections from your local museum or library service.

7 Encouraging the children to look at the objects is a useful start, but they will get more out of this if you organise it around some practical activities which help to develop their powers of observation. These might include drawing the objects, describing an object to another child who must then pick out the object from the collection, writing descriptions of the objects for labels or for catalogue cards.

8 Encourage the children to answer questions. What do the objects look and feel like? What are they made of? What were they used for? Who made them? What makes them work? How old are they? How could you find out more about them? Do they do the job they are supposed to do?

9 What do the objects tell us about the people who used them? Children might do some writing, drawing or role play, imagining themselves as the owners of different objects.

10 Children might find a mystery object connected with travel for the others to draw, write about and identify. Children can compare the objects in the book with objects they find or know about.

11 If you have an exhibition, try pairing old objects with their nearest modern counterparts. Talk about each pair. Some useful questions might be: How can you tell which is older? Which objects have changed most over time? Why? What do you think of the older objects? What would people have thought of them when they were new? Can you test how well the objects work? Is the modern version better than the older version?

12 Make a time-line using your objects. You might find the time-line at the back of this book useful. You could include pictures in your time-line and other markers to help the children gain a sense of chronology. Use your time-line to bring out the elements of *change* (eg. the gradual development of motor transport and the electrification of the railways, modern problems of pollution) and *continuity* (eg. the need for individual and public transport).

History Mysteries

First published 1992
A & C Black (Publishers) Limited
35 Bedford Row, London WC1R 4JH

ISBN 0–7136–3492–8

© 1992 A & C Black (Publishers) Limited

A CIP catalogue record for this book is available
from the British Library.

Acknowledgements

The authors and publisher would like to thank the following for the
loan of artefacts from their collections:
John Cockcroft (curator of the Industrial Museum, Wollaton Hall, Nottingham),
Andrew Hales, Dick Buckingham, Rosie Sacker
(librarian, National Tramway Museum, Critch, Derbyshire),
Rodney Cousins (curator, Museum of Lincolnshire Life, Lincoln),
Andrew Burton (guard, Loughborough Central Station,
Great Central Steam Railway, Loughborough, Leicestershire),
Royal Army Veterinary Corps (Leicestershire).

Filmset by August Filmsetting, Haydock, St Helens
Printed and bound in Italy by L.E.G.O.